BOOK 1

CHRISTMAS HITS for TEENS

11 GRADED SELECTIONS
FOR EARLY INTERMEDIATE PIANISTS

ARRANGED BY DAN COATES

The *Christmas Hits for Teens* series presents carefully leveled, accessible arrangements for the teenage pianist. This series provides students with the fun opportunity to develop their technique and musicianship while performing their favorite Christmas songs and carols.

CONTENTS

ALL I WANT FOR CHRISTMAS IS MY TWO FRONT TEETH 2

AWAY IN A MANGER 4

DECK THE HALLS 6

FELIZ NAVIDAD 7

GOD REST YE MERRY, GENTLEMEN 10

HARK! THE HERALD ANGELS SING 12

JOY TO THE WORLD 24

O CHRISTMAS TREE 14

RUDOLPH, THE RED-NOSED REINDEER 16

SANTA CLAUS IS COMIN' TO TOWN 19

TOYLAND 22

Produced by
Alfred Music
P.O. Box 10003
Van Nuys, CA 91410-0003
alfred.com

Printed in USA.

ISBN-10: 1-4706-3884-3
ISBN-13: 978-1-4706-3884-9

ALL I WANT FOR CHRISTMAS IS MY TWO FRONT TEETH

Words and Music by Don Gardner
Arr. Dan Coates

AWAY IN A MANGER

James R. Murray
Arr. Dan Coates

Slowly, with expression

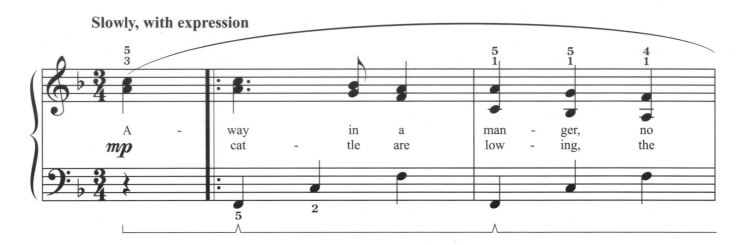

A - way in a man - ger, no the
cat - tle are low - ing, the

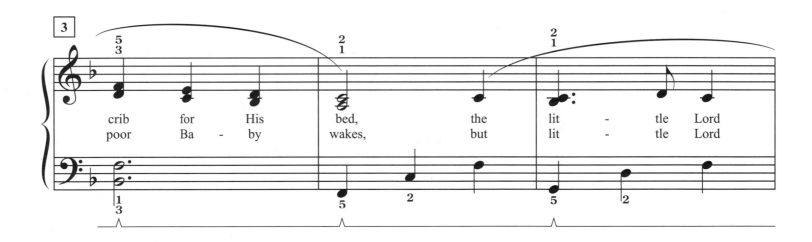

crib for His bed, the lit - tle Lord
poor Ba - by wakes, but lit - tle Lord

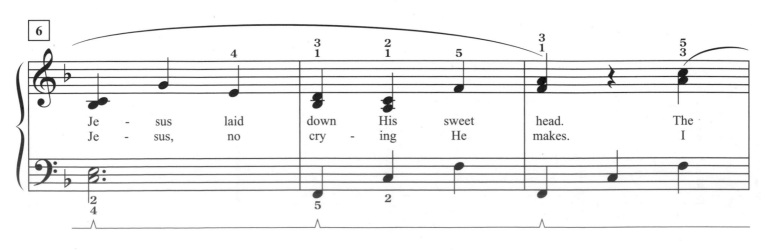

Je - sus laid down His sweet head. The
Je - sus, no cry - ing He makes. I

DECK THE HALLS

Traditional Welsh Carol
Arr. Dan Coates

FELIZ NAVIDAD

Words and Music by José Feliciano
Arr. Dan Coates

Fe - liz Na - vi - dad. Pros - pe - ro a - ño y fe - li - ci - dad.

I want to wish you a Mer - ry Christ - mas.

I want to wish you a Mer - ry Christ - mas. I want to wish you a

Mer - ry Christ - mas from the bot - tom of my heart.

GOD REST YE MERRY, GENTLEMEN

Traditional English Carol
Arr. Dan Coates

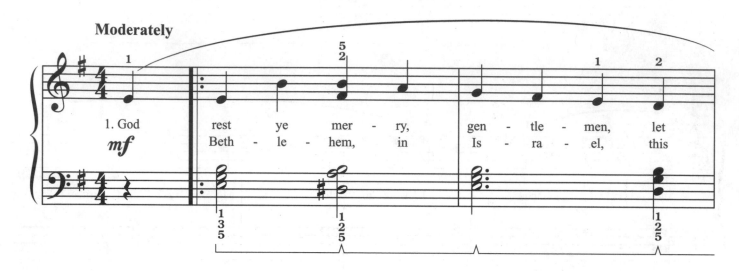

HARK! THE HERALD ANGELS SING

Words by Charles Wesley
Music by Felix Mendelssohn
Arr. Dan Coates

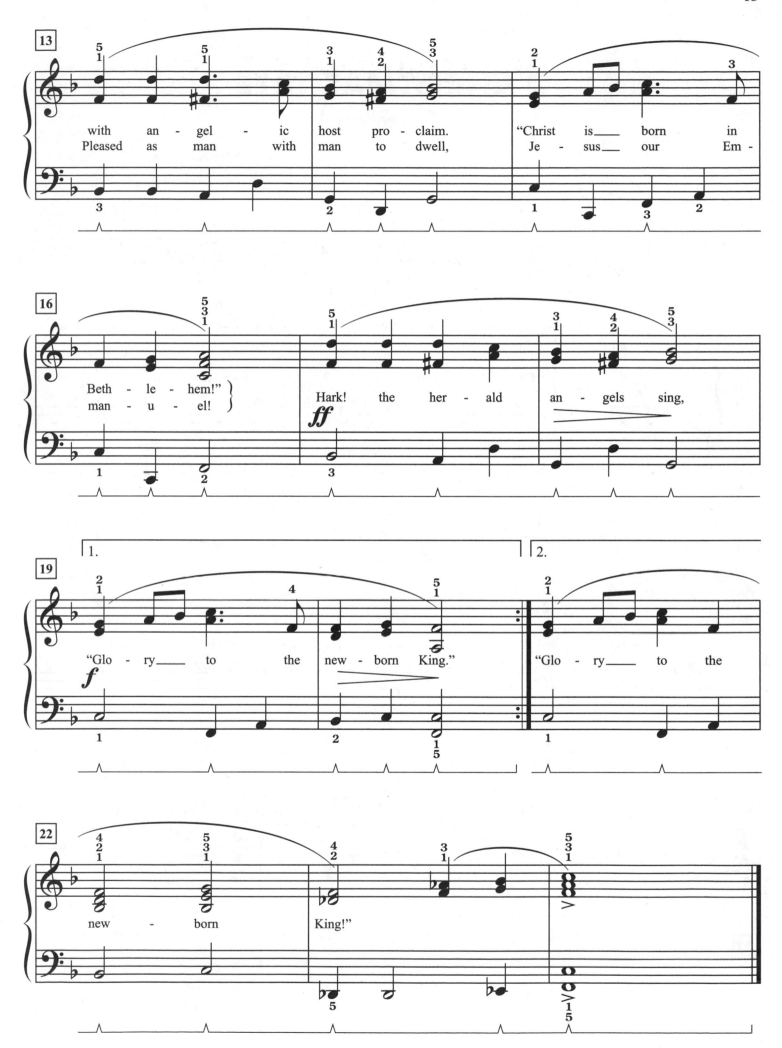

13

O CHRISTMAS TREE
(O Tannenbaum)

Traditional German Carol
Arr. Dan Coates

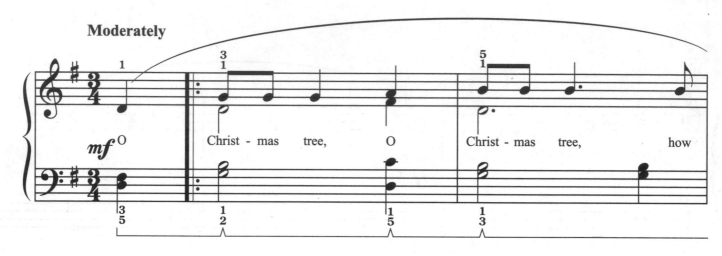

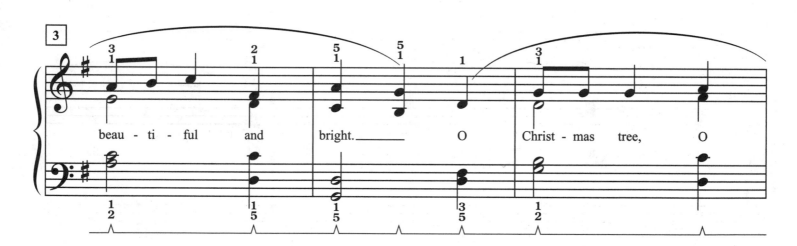

RUDOLPH, THE RED-NOSED REINDEER

Words and Music by Johnny Marks
Arr. Dan Coates

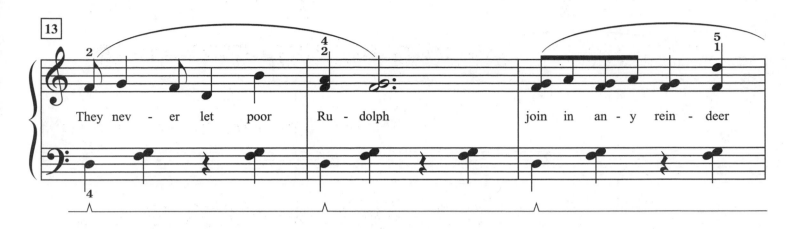

They nev - er let poor Ru - dolph join in an - y rein - deer

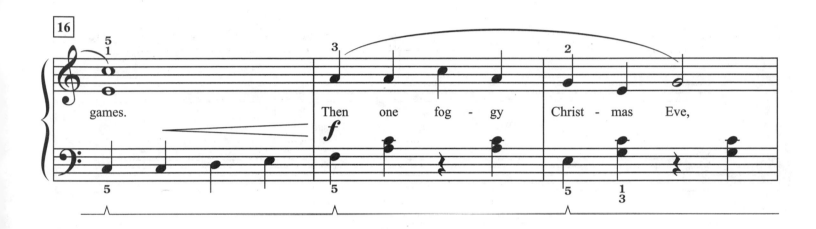

games. Then one fog - gy Christ - mas Eve,

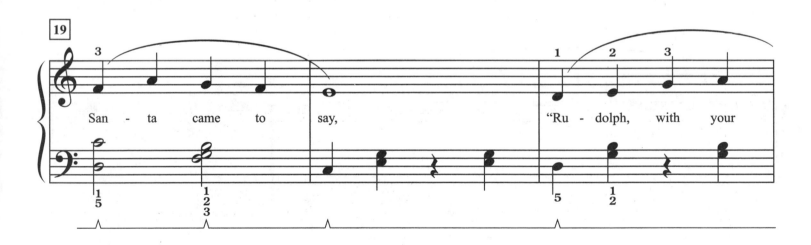

San - ta came to say, "Ru - dolph, with your

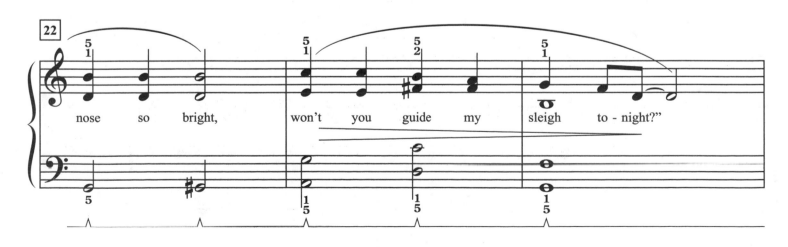

nose so bright, won't you guide my sleigh to - night?"

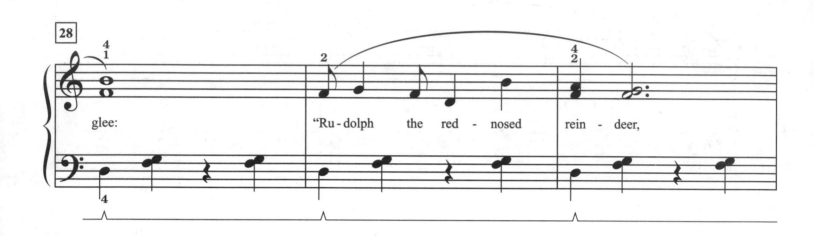

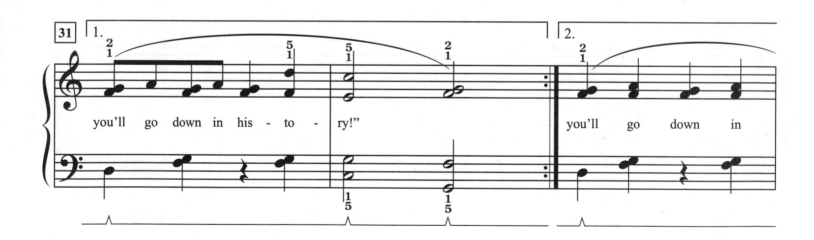

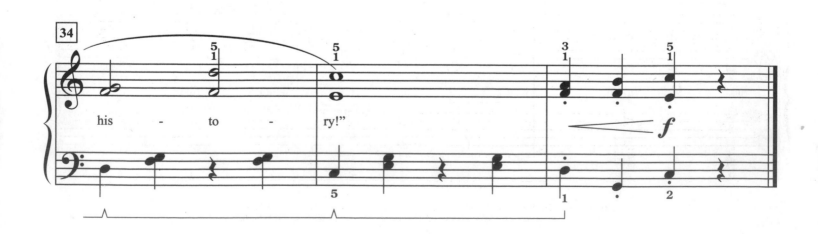

SANTA CLAUS IS COMIN' TO TOWN

Words by Haven Gillespie
Music by J. Fred Coots
Arr. Dan Coates

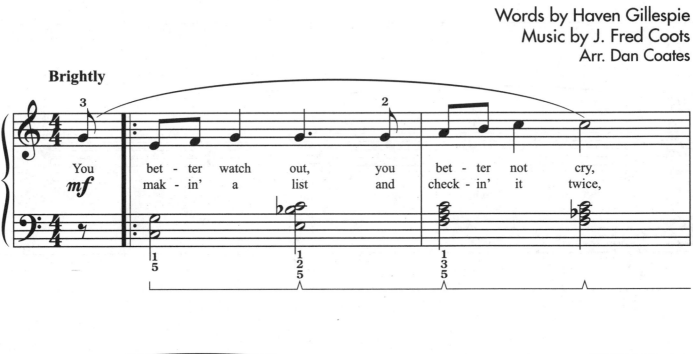

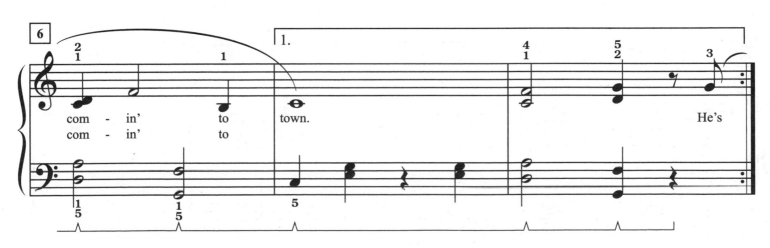

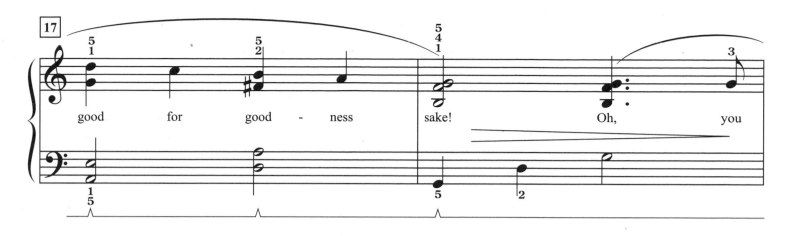

good   for   good - ness   sake!   Oh,   you

bet - ter watch   out,   you   bet - ter not   cry,

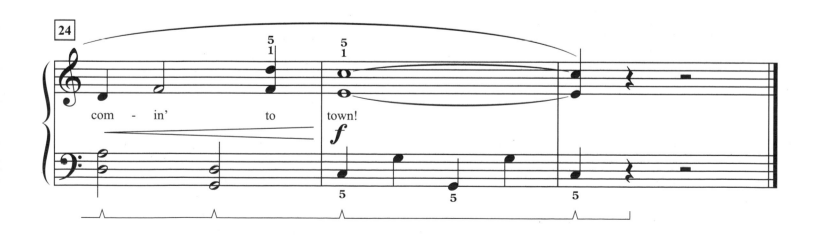

bet - ter not pout, I'm   tell - in' you   why: San - ta Claus is

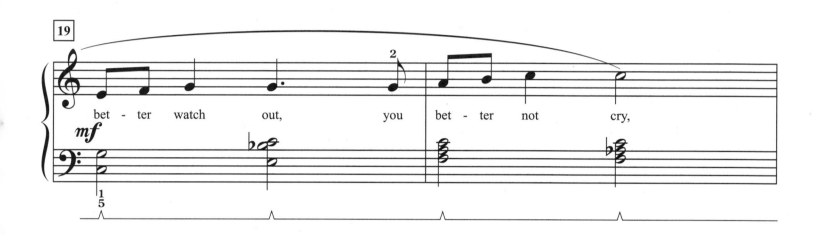

com - in'   to   town!

TOYLAND

Words by Glen MacDonough
Music by Victor Herbert
Arr. Dan Coates

Slowly, with expression

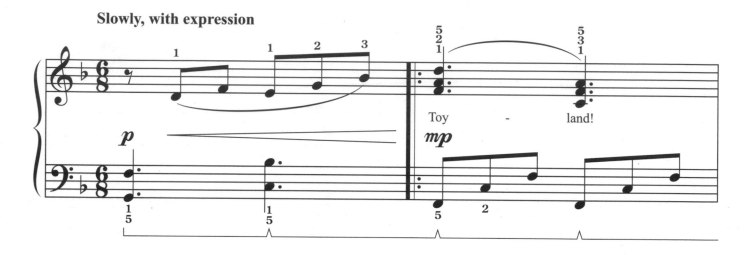

Toy - land!

Toy - land! Beau - ti - ful girl and boy - land,

while you dwell with - in it, you are

JOY TO THE WORLD

Words by Isaac Watts
Music by Lowell Mason
Arr. Dan Coates